T0326921

# WHEN YOU WANT TO WANT TO YELL AT GOD

THE BOOK OF JOB

**Other titles in
the Transformative Word series:**

*God Behind the Scenes: The Book of Esther*
by Wayne Barkhuizen

*Revealing the Heart of Prayer: The Gospel of Luke*
By Craig G. Bartholomew

*Cutting Ties with Darkness: 2 Corinthians*
by John D. Barry

*Between the Cross and the Throne: The Book of Revelation*
by Matthew Emerson

# WHEN YOU WANT TO YELL AT GOD

## THE BOOK OF JOB

### TRANSFORMATIVE WORD

CRAIG G. BARTHOLOMEW

Author and Series Editor

LEXHAM PRESS

Series Editor: Craig G. Bartholomew
Lexham Editorial Team: Lynnea Fraser, Rebecca Brant,
    Abigail Stocker
Cover Design: Christine Gerhart
Back Cover Design: Brittany Schrock
Typesetting: ProjectLuz.com

The crucible for silver and the furnace for gold,
but the LORD tests the heart.

Proverbs 17:3

# TABLE OF CONTENTS

# INTRODUCTION

A student once asked Brevard Childs how to become a better exegete of the Bible. Childs replied, "Become a deeper person!" Job is one biblical book that is both about its main character becoming a deeper person and an invitation to the reader to be formed by God.

## OUTLINE FOR THE BOOK OF JOB

1. Introduction: Job, God, and the Accuser (Job 1–2)

2. Dialogues between Job and His Friends (Job 3–26)

3. Monologues of Job, Elihu, and God (Job 27–41)

4. Conclusion (Job 42)

## Overview

The book of Job is one of the best examples of biblical literary art. The book is primarily poetry with a narrated introduction (Job 1-2) and conclusion (Job 42). The introduction sets up the discussion that follows in the poetry by drawing attention to Job, a "blameless and upright" man "who feared God and turned away from evil" (1:1 NRSV). God is pleased with Job, but "the Accuser" (Hebrew *ha-satan*) insists Job's faith is superficial and would not stand up to the test if his health and wealth were taken away (1:9–11; 2:4–5). God permits the Accuser (that is, Satan) to bring disaster on Job and his family, destroying everything in the world that he holds dear—possessions, people, and his physical well-being. At the end of Job 2, three friends—Eliphaz, Bildad, and Zophar—come to comfort Job in his time of distress. The poetry in Job 3–31 contains the dialogue among these three and Job as they consider the possible causes of Job's misfortune and suggest ways for Job to regain favor with God. In Job 32–37, another man, Elihu, offers his advice to Job. Finally, Job 38–41 records God's response to Job, in which God emphasizes his divine sovereignty over all creation but never explicitly explains to Job why he suffered. Job is humbled by the divine encounter, and the book concludes with God restoring Job's family and fortune (Job 42).

### WHEN IS JOB'S STORY SET?

It is unclear when the book was written, but the story appears to be set during patriarchal times (contemporary with Abraham, Isaac, and Jacob). Evidence for this includes Job's practice of sacrifice and the fact that his wealth is measured in livestock, as well as certain linguistic elements.

## The Theological Center of Job

The ethical idea of "what goes around comes around" (often called "karma" or "poetic justice") has a big influence on popular culture. A modern example is the angry driver who cuts off another car and immediately has an accident (like in many viral videos). The idea is not new. Even in ancient times people believed that there was a simple cause-and-effect relationship between behavior and experience. Suffering was believed to be a punishment for bad behavior, while prosperity was the reward for good behavior. If you were a wicked person, eventually you (or your descendants) would "get what's coming to you." For example, in John 9:2 Jesus' disciples see a man blind from birth and ask, "Who sinned, this man or his parents, that he was born blind?" In that passage and elsewhere (e.g., Luke 13:1–5), Jesus rejects the idea that sin and suffering can be so closely connected, in such a cause-and-effect relationship. However, biblical Wisdom literature is sometimes thought to encourage such thinking with statements like Psalm 7:14–16 or Proverbs 26:27.[1]

> See how they conceive evil, and are pregnant with mischief, and bring forth lies. They make a pit, digging it out, and fall into the hole that they have made. Their mischief returns upon their own heads, and on their own heads their violence descends (Psa 7:14–16 NRSV).

> Whoever digs a pit will fall into it, and a stone will come back on the one who starts it rolling (Prov 26:27 NRSV).

Such verses remind us that sin and folly can and do lead to suffering. But the book of Job reminds us that not all suffering is the result of sin.

Since Job's three friends continually affirm the idea that Job's suffering must somehow be connected to bad behavior (either his own or that of his family), the book of Job has often been read as a crisis-induced response to conventional wisdom, especially the straightforward cause-and-effect theology found in many biblical proverbs. This oversimplified understanding of Job (and Proverbs too) results in a loss of the rich theological message of biblical Wisdom literature.[2] As I will argue below, Job does not represent a crisis in proverbial type wisdom, and Proverbs itself recognizes that while wisdom does lead to blessing, the path to wisdom may be difficult.

Proverbs 17:3 provides a clue to the overall purpose of biblical wisdom teaching (which includes Proverbs and Job). The proverb reads: "The crucible for silver and the furnace for gold; but the LORD tests the heart." The metalworking imagery evokes rigorous formation; silver and gold have to be exposed to high temperatures and smelted down before they can be transformed into jewelry. The wise writer of Proverbs is well aware that the path to wisdom might lead through the furnace! Proverbs repeatedly identifies *the heart* as the center of a person. Thus, what is in view here is spiritual and moral formation down to the deepest levels of

> Proverbs teaches that the road to wisdom may lead through intense testing, suffering, and purification. And this teaching is precisely what we find in Job.

an individual's being. Rather than offering a simplistic view of wisdom as an easily acquired technique that automatically leads to blessing, Proverbs teaches that the road to wisdom may lead through intense testing, suffering, and purification.

And this teaching is precisely what we find in Job. The book of Job teaches how godly character results from refining in the furnace of *formation*.

**SUGGESTED READING**

☐    Job 1–2

☐    Psalm 7

☐    Proverbs 1:1–19

## Reflection

Do you usually read biblical proverbs as always true or just generally true?

_____

_____

_____

How do you think blessing and suffering are related?

_____

_____

_____

# THE PORTRAIT
# OF JOB

If the person of Job feels familiar to us, we should de-familiarize ourselves with him. Job 1:1 records that he lived in Uz, apparently somewhere between Edom (southern Jordan) and Babylon (south-central Iraq). This, surprisingly, is a story of a non-Israelite living far away from the promised land. The biblical text also describes Job as devout, as one who "feared God and shunned evil" (1:1). In 1:1–5 the name for God is the generic "Elohim." Thus, it is not immediately clear which god/s Job served. But beginning in 1:6, the common name for God switches mainly to "Yahweh"—the distinctive name of the covenant God of Israel. So Job is clearly identified as serving and fearing Yahweh.

Throughout the Bible, "fearing God" is the classic expression for being wise, and the book begins by describing Job as an incomparably wise and righteous man who fears Israel's covenant God (Yahweh) but who lives in the East apart from Israel's known habitation. Job was also blessed with great wealth, and 1:3 describes him as "the greatest man among all the people of the East."

## WHERE WAS UZ?

Job's hometown is difficult to place. Job 1:3 notes that Uz was in "the east," but no further geographical information is given in the book. Other biblical mentions of the word may put it near Edom to the south  (Lam 4:21) or Aram to the north (Gen 10:22–23).

This is how Job appeared to his fellow citizens, but how does he look to God? In chapters 1 and 2 the narrative moves back and forth between heaven and earth. Intriguingly in 1:8 Yahweh himself draws Job to Satan's attention and describes him in the same terms the narrator does (compare 1:1 with 1:8). Satan questions this depiction of Job, arguing that Job only fears God because God protects him and blesses him.

In this way, Job's faith is brought into question: Why exactly does he serve God? What are his motivations? In other words, the encounter between Yahweh and Satan moves the focus of the story from appearance to reality at the deepest level—the level of the heart.

Indeed, there appears to be a touch of irony in the description of Job

> The encounter between Yahweh and Satan moves the focus of the story from appearance to reality at the deepest level—the level of the heart.

in 1:1–5. The description here is that of a man who is almost too good to believe, which is confirmed in Job's practices as described in 1:5. Job allowed his sons to host regular feasts, but after each period of feasting, he had his children pass through a purification ritual. And lest his children might "have sinned and cursed God in their hearts," he would offer a burnt offering for each one of them. Job had a sense that all might not be well with his children, and he feared that they might have committed the really serious sin of cursing God, a sin meriting the death penalty in Israel. Perhaps all was not as well as it appeared with Job's children, but his greatest fear appears to be that their behavior would bring God's judgment rather than his ongoing blessing. Therefore, part of Job's religion was motivated by an unhealthy anxiety and fear.

Let's look more closely at Satan's words; there is more here than meets the eye, some—albeit partial and distorted—truth, just as there was in the serpent's speech in Genesis. In Genesis 3 the serpent correctly stated that Adam and Eve would not die on the day they ate the forbidden fruit. Of course, in a greater sense they did die, but not on a physical level. And so in Job, too, Satan correctly touches on Job's mixed motivations within his religion.

God grants Satan permission to put Job to the test, though within limits (Job 1:12; 2:6), first through the destruction of his children and his wealth (1:13–19) and then through a painful disease (2:7). After the destruction of his children and his wealth, Job exhibits extraordinary faith:

> Naked I came from my mother's womb,
> and naked I will depart.
> The LORD gave and the LORD has taken away,
> may the name of the LORD be praised (1:21).

Similarly, when Job is struck down with an awful disease and his wife urges him to "curse God and die!" (2:9)—probably suggesting a form of suicide, since to curse God would bring his ultimate judgment—Job responds, "Shall we accept good from God, and not trouble?" (2:10).

We might think the book of Job should end here—with faith triumphing over adversity. Instead, the book continues for another 40 chapters, as Job struggles to come to terms with what has happened to him. At the end of Job 2, his three friends—Eliphaz, Bildad, and Zophar—arrive and wisely sit with him in silence for seven days, mourning Job's losses. The friends start off so well: Immediately they hear of Job's distress; they travel great distances to be with him; and when they see him and can hardly recognize him, they discern the extent of his sufferings (2:11–13).

In chapter 3 Job plunges into despair, cursing the day of his birth and wishing he could undo the very fiber of creation. In his first speech, Job curses the day of his birth, the "day," the "light," and the night, strategically reversing the order of God's creative work in Genesis 1.[1] As Job falls apart, he inadvertently reveals important things about himself. For example, he imagines that if he died, he would retain his high position in society

> As Job falls apart, he inadvertently reveals important things about himself.

and be with kings, counselors, and wealthy rulers (3:14).

In 3:25 he acknowledges that what has happened to him has fulfilled his worst fears. The very things his religion was designed to protect him from have happened. Even as we sympathize with Job, we see that his suffering is touching on the very areas of his life that most needed attention if he was to become truly wise. There is nothing pleasant about this and his suffering is unimaginable; yet, despite Satan or through Satan, God is at work in his formation of Job.

Job's realization of his deepest fears—of that from which he most sought to protect himself—indicates that there is more going on with Job than simply meaningless suffering. A psychologist friend of mine, Brenda Stephenson, calls this "creative suffering." This title does not for a moment detract from the sheer hell of Job's experience, but it signifies that a transformative process is at work amid the hell. Deep suffering is terribly slow and protracted, just like Job 3–41. If you find 3–41 slow, repetitive, and, frankly, a bit of a drag, then remember that this book performs on the reader the experience of suffering; it is exhausting, tiring, and feels like an endless painful cycle. It's relentless.

> This book performs on the reader the experience of suffering; it is exhausting, tiring, and feels like an endless painful cycle. It's relentless.

In 42:5 Job looks back and describes his journey: "My ears had heard of you, but now my eyes have seen you." Job is on a journey from being wise to being wise at a much deeper level of his being. It is a journey of depth formation and one that moves deeply into God; of course, in Christian spirituality these two go together. His suffering does come to an end. He is transformed and his fortunes are restored (42:1–17). But 3–41 remind us that there is no shortcut in a journey of transformation. We all want to be saints, but few of us are prepared for the journey it requires!

Job's journey involves despair, physical and mental suffering, counseling, anger, desperate appeals to God, and anything-but-passive waiting. He entered a tunnel of darkness and had no idea where it led.

### SUGGESTED READING

- [ ] Job 1–3; 42
- [ ] Appendix A: "Fearing God in the Old Testament" by Miles Custis
- [ ] Appendix B: "Satan in the Old Testament and the Serpent of Genesis 3" by Michael S. Heiser

## Reflection

Job was regarded as very wise by his fellow citizens and "church members." But was he really?

At the deepest level, what motivates you to serve God?

_____

_____

Are there any unhelpful motives that you need to gently surface and hold before God, asking him to help you serve him because he is God?

_____

_____

_____

# THE PORTRAITS OF GOD AMONG JOB'S FRIENDS

Years ago a British doctor, Sheila Cassidy, went to serve as a doctor in Chile. She gave medical aid to a government opponent and was arrested, tortured, and eventually released and returned to the UK.[1] I heard her speak in Cheltenham, and she made the important point that we need images of God that are *adequate for the journey of life* with all its challenges.

This is especially true of suffering since it turns ours lives upside down and we feel helpless, with no idea what God is up to. In such contexts, it becomes all the more important that we hold on to healthy concepts of God. In this respect, it is fascinating to see what views Job and his friends have of God.

Suffering often drives us to look for help, and today that usually means seeking counseling. In the last century or so counseling has exploded as a profession and many of us turn to professional counselors when in trouble, when suffering comes knocking at our doors. Turning to others for help is a natural and good thing; but times of suffering are also vulnerable times, and we need wise counselors with healthy views of God to help us on our journeys.

> Times of suffering are also vulnerable times, and we need wise counselors with healthy views of God to help us on our journeys.

At first it appears that Job's friends are model counselors. They are older, influential people, and once they hear of Job's troubles, their response is impeccable. The take leave from their busy and important lives, travel long distances, discern the extent of Job's suffering, and sit with him in silence for seven days of lament and mourning. Furthermore, in their discussions they all consider God with the utmost seriousness. When Job starts to bare his tortured soul in Job 3 they soon begin to respond, and then we discover that these good friends have unhelpful views of God and his ways. The seemingly endless speeches stretch from 3–37, until God comes on the scene and addresses Job in 38–41.

### WHO SAID THAT?

It can be easy to lose track of who is speaking during the long speeches of Job and his friends, but the author has in fact helpfully organized their speeches in cycles that include the criticisms of Job's friends and his responses to them. Here is one way of organizing these cycles: cycle 1 (Job 3–14), cycle 2 (Job 15–21), cycle 3 (Job 22–31), Elihu's four speeches (Job 32–37).

Having been provoked by Job's outbursts of agony and despair (see also 4:2; 8:2; 11:2–3), Job's friends enter the dialogue. Their responses make for fascinating reading. They line up to defend God against Job's outbursts and to affirm a *mechanical*, automatic view of what has been called the act-consequence theme in biblical wisdom. Proverbs in particular and biblical wisdom in general teach that obedience leads to blessing and sin to judgment. But, as we noted above, even Proverbs demonstrates a much more nuanced view of this theme. The friends make a great mistake in viewing God as operating in a simple, mechanistic fashion. The brutality of this approach is evident in Bildad's first speech. In 8:4 he states unequivocally that he knows why Job's children died: "When your children sinned against him, he gave them over to the penalty of their sin." One by one, Job's friends urge him to be completely honest about the sin in his life that is supposedly causing his miseries.

The climax of Eliphaz's argument is found in Job 22. In 22:5 he asks, "Is not your wickedness great? Are not your sins endless?" And then in 22:6–9 he lists a series of sins that he accuses Job of committing. His conclusion: "That is why snares are all around you, why sudden peril terrifies you, why it is so dark that you cannot see, and why a flood of water covers you." Eliphaz's solution is found in 22:21–30, where he says Job must repent of his sins and call to God.

In Job 20 Zophar rants about the fate of the wicked. He concludes in 20:29 with: "Such is the fate God allots the wicked, the heritage appointed for them by God."

The point of Bildad's case is found in Job 25. In 25:4 he asks, "How can a mortal be righteous before God? How can one born of a woman be pure?" Bildad finds it unthinkable that Job can keep protesting his innocence.

How do Job's friends view God? There is much about their view that is thoroughly orthodox. They have a biblical view of God as transcendent and yet deeply involved in his world. They recognize that God is just. They rightly see human life as lived before the face of God, and they know that God hears and answers prayer. They understand that God reveals himself to humans (see also 33:14–15).

> Their God is reduced to their mechanistic theology. They may appear orthodox, but Job finds them of no help in his torment.

In 4:12–17 Eliphaz describes a mystical experience in which a word of "God" comes to him. But they have no sense of God as God, a God whose ways are often unexpected and inscrutable. Their God is reduced to their mechanistic theology. They may appear orthodox, but Job finds them of no help in his torment. In 16:2 he describes his friends as "miserable comforters"!

The three friends are old and mature, but a young man has been observing the dialogue; once he sees that the three friends have made no progress with Job, he can no longer contain himself. In 32:1 we read that the three stopped answering Job because "he was righteous in his own eyes." The younger Elihi (see also 32:6–9) can no longer contain his anger because Job is justifying himself in his own eyes rather than God's (32:2). The young man, however, provides more of the same sort of advice, seeking to defend God against Job's outbursts.

Then God gives a verdict on the friends' advice in 42:7:

> After the LORD had said these things to Job, he said to Eliphaz the Temanite, "I am angry with you and your two friends, because you have not spoken of me what is right, as my servant Job has."

God commands Eliphaz to offer a burnt offering and to have Job pray for him so that God will not deal with him "according to your folly. You have not spoken of me what is right, as my servant Job has" (42:8).

The repetition of "you have not spoken of me what is right, as my servant Job has" makes God's view of the friends' advice clear. It is not wisdom but folly! What was wrong with the friends' view of God? Note that God says to Eliphaz twice, "You have not spoken of *me* what is right." The friends assume that God, being wholly good and all powerful, would never allow Job's sort of suffering to befall a righteous man, but they are deceived. As Édouard Dhorme says, "His friends seek to apply normal solutions to the exceptional case."[2] Job protests and rails against the mystery of what has befallen him; the friends, however, assume that their mechanistic theology can penetrate that mystery and explain Job's circumstances. The result, as we see in their speeches, is cruel and vindictive counsel to a man experiencing despair and feeling lost amid his undeserved suffering. Can you imagine saying to a man who has recently lost all his children, "When your children sinned against him [God], he gave them over to the penalty of their sin"?

**SUGGESTED READING**

☐ If you have time, read the whole of Job 4–37. If not, choose one of Job's friends and read his speeches and Job's responses.

## Reflection

Choose one of the friends from Job 4–37 to focus on. What do you make of his arguments? What view of God does he present?

_____

_____

_____

Read through Job's responses to this friend. What are his major points?

_____

_____

_____

Imagine you are one of Job's friends. What would you say to Job?

_____

_____

_____

Imagine you are Job. What would you say to the friend whose speeches you read?

_____

_____

_____

# JOB'S VIEW OF GOD

We know that Job's friends held a false view of God, but how could God so readily affirm Job as having spoken correctly about him (42:7–8)? Does this refer only to Job's speech in 42:1–6 or does it refer to all that he has said in the book? God's indictment of Eliphaz places the friends' words in contrast with what Job has said. Thus, God's verdict appears to apply to *all* that Job has said and not just his confession in 42:1–6.

How should we characterize Job's speeches? A major element is *protest*. As Job says in 7:11, "I will not keep silent; I will speak out in the anguish of my spirit, I will complain in the bitterness of my soul." The philosopher Alvin Plantinga points out that Job's problem can be understood in two ways.[1] The first, common interpretation is the intellectual one: Job protests because he cannot understand why God would allow an innocent person to suffer. As Martin Buber perceptively notes, "Job cannot forego either his own truth or God."[2] The second possibility is that Job is angry and disagrees with what God is doing. God may have reasons, but Job, in effect, says, "I don't give a fig for those reasons, and I detest what he is doing!"[3] These two responses are not antithetical and combine in

Job's tormented protests to God.[4] It is not that Job sees himself as sinless; in 7:17–21 he fires off a series of questions at God, one of which is "Why do you not pardon my offenses and forgive my sins?" Job is open to the fact that he is a sinner, but he cannot wrap his mind around the lack of proportion between any of his sins and what God

> Job is open to the fact that he is a sinner, but he cannot wrap his mind around the lack of proportion between any of his sins and what God has allowed to happen to him.

has allowed to happen to him. In this sense, Buber is surely right: "Job cannot forego either his own truth or God." In Job's words to his friends, "Till I die, I will not deny my integrity" (27:5). The result is excruciating tension, despair, and rage.

As we find in the Psalms, God wants his people to bring their difficulties, problems, and complaints to him, and this is what Job does. Job's friends theologize about his situation, whereas Job lives it in all its ugliness before God (see, for example, 7:7: "Remember, O God"; 7:19–21; 16:7–8; 30:20–31). A major difference between Job and his friends is that Job addresses God directly and appeals to him, whereas the friends merely talk about Job's situation. Job's God is one to whom he can direct strong protest, whereas the friends' God is one who has already revealed truth and that truth just needs to be applied to Job's situation. As Robert Alter notes: "Job's cosmic poetry, unlike that of the Friends, has a certain energy of vision, as though it proceeded from some immediate perception of the great things it reports."[5]

In terms of Job's view of God, he:

- recognizes God as ultimately behind his situation (3:23; 6:4);

- knows that God is the creator and sovereign over his creation (9:1–10; see also 28);

- experiences God as completely absent in his sufferings (9:11; in 23:17 he describes his experience as one of "thick darkness");

- experiences his life of suffering as meaningless (10:18–22); and

- wants to bring God to court to force God to answer his case against him (10:2; 13:3) but recognizes that God is of a different order entirely to humankind (9:14–20, 32–35).

Job experiences God's actions in his life as a complete mystery, and to his credit he lives this mystery in all its agony before his friends and God.

Job 28 is an extraordinary poem about wisdom. Because of its serenity and beauty, scholars have questioned its place between Job's raging in 26–27 and 29–31 and its authenticity as one of Job's speeches. In my view, its juxtaposition between Job's rants is appropriate since this is how extreme suffering goes—moving from despair to insight and sanity, and then plunging back into the hell. In this context, Job 28 is extraordinary and anticipates the arrival of God on the scene in Job 38. Whereas Proverbs starts with the fear of the Lord as the key to knowing the world, Job 28 starts from the other end, as it were, first acknowledging the extraordinary feats that humankind is capable of in mining the depths of the earth for precious metals (28:1-11). However, despite humankind's great abilities, neither they nor the personified creation know the way to the source of wisdom (28:12-22). Even those great boundaries of death and destruction can say, "Only a rumor of it has reached our ears" (28:22). It is God alone who knows the source of wisdom, for it lies in him. He is the creator and humankind is the creature, so: "The fear of the Lord—that is wisdom" (28:23-28).

## JOB 28: AN INTERLUDE ON WISDOM

Job 28 is a poem that asks, "Where shall wisdom be found?" It is unclear whether it is spoken by Job or is a self-contained poem added by the narrator. It includes a description of the lengths people go to when searching for gold and other valuable resources (28:1−11). It then turns to wisdom, showing wisdom's value and questioning its accessibility (28:12−22). Finally, it reveals God as the source of wisdom (28:23−28).

God arrives on the scene in Job 38. Long has Job waited for this, but he could never have expected the answer he receives from "out of the storm" (38:1). Ironically, God's *answer* is a series of more than 80 rhetorical *questions*. The two lists of questions are divided by Job's short reply in 40:3-5. God immediately begins his speech with questions:

> Then the Lord *answered* Job *out of the storm.*
> He said:

> Who is this that darkens my counsel with
> words without knowledge?
> Gird up your loins like a man,
> I will question you, and you shall declare to
> me (38:1–3).

The word "storm" (se'arah) appears here for the first time in Job, and it is used again in 40:6. As Lindsay Wilson suggests, the "storm cloaks the fierce otherness of the presence of God in his fullness in the midst of the world of human experience ... "[6] In his own way, God does indeed reply to Job. Alter notes of God's speech:

> When God finally answers Job out of the whirlwind, he responds with an order of poetry formally allied to Job's own remarkable poetry, but larger in scope and greater in power... That is, God picks up many of Job's key images, especially from the death-wish poem with which Job began (Chapter 3) and his discourse is shaped by a powerful movement of intensification, coupled with an implicitly narrative sweep from the creation to the play of natural forces to the teeming world of animal life.[7]

Michael Fox's analysis of the questions that make up the bulk of God's speech reveals a whole range of techniques at work in God's reply to Job.[8] The questions are of three types: (1) "Who?" questions, which point back to God's power (e.g., "Who shut up the sea behind doors?"; 38:8); (2) "What?" questions, which emphasize the breadth of God's power (e.g., "What is the way to the abode of light?"; 38:19); and (3) "Have you ever?" or "Can you?" questions, which reinforce the limits of human power and knowledge (e.g., "Have you entered the storehouses of the snow?"; 38:22).

Job is confronted with the power of God, with the huge difference between God as creator and himself as created, with the omniscience of God and the limits of his own knowledge. In the middle of God's speeches, Job responds briefly (40:3–5). He acknowledges the power of God's evidence and his own finitude: "I am unworthy," or more literally "I am humbled" (40:4a). This is proba-

> Job is confronted with the power of God, with the huge difference between God as creator and himself as created, with the omniscience of God and the limits of his own knowledge.

bly not a confession of guilt, since Job is aware of his innocence as far as the suffering is concerned, but a confession of his creatureliness before the omnipotent creator. Job also realizes that although he has been given space to speak—the very thing he had wanted for so long—it is now appropriate to remain silent: "I put my hand over my mouth" (40:4).

After Job's short speech, God returns to his questions and to two unusual descriptions of the Behemoth (40:15–24) and the Leviathan (41:1–34).

> Look at Behemoth, which I made along with you and which feeds on grass like an ox. What strength it has in its loins, what power in the muscles of its belly! ...

> Can you pull in Leviathan with a fishhook
> or tie down its tongue with a rope? Can you
> put a cord through its nose or pierce its jaw
> with a hook?

Behemoth is the plural word for "beast" (*behemah*) and is the same word used for the first creatures on the land in Genesis 1:24, typically considered cattle. It is common nowadays, however, to interpret this as a reference to the crocodile or the hippopotamus; the fact that it "feeds on grass like an ox" (Job 40:15) makes it more likely that it refers to the hippopotamus. Leviathan is also referred to by Job in 3:8 and in other Old Testament passages concerned with the mysterious nature of creation and justice (see, for example, Pss 74:14; 104:26; Isa 27:1). As in Psalms 74 and 104, the use of Leviathan here in Job could refer to the whale as the great creature of the deep. The reference in Isaiah 27, however, portrays a "coiling" or "twisting" serpent creature. The mythical connections with water, chaos, and the deep cannot be ruled out, nor can the personification of death.[9] Together the Behemoth and the Leviathan reinforce the overall message of the divine speeches: God's creation is vast, diverse, and mysterious—way beyond human control and yet easily within *his* control. The poetry of the questions accentuates the strength of God's answers to Job.

> God's creation is vast, diverse, and mysterious—way beyond human control and yet easily within *his* control.

But whereas Job's intensities are centripetal and necessarily egocentric, God's intensities carry us back and forth through the pulsating vital movements of the whole created world. The culmination of the poem God speaks is not a cry of self or a dream of self snuffed out, but the terrible beauty of the Leviathan, on the uncanny borderline between zoology and mythology, where what is fierce and strange, beyond the conquest of man, is the climactic manifestation of a splendidly providential creation that merely anthropomorphic notions cannot grasp.[10]

God's speeches alert us to two fundamental truths about God. First, he is God and we are creatures. Job acknowledges this in Job 42:3, referring back to God's penetrating question in 38:2 and its parallel in 42:3: "Surely I spoke of things I did not understand, things too wonderful for me to know." Second, God's powerful and often mysterious rule of the universe, while utterly sovereign (see 42:2), is caring, with its eye on the well-being of his whole creation. God satisfies the land with rain (38:27); he feeds the lion (38:39) and the raven (39:41); he provides the wild donkey with a home and food (39:5–8). He also provides freedom and the "wisdom" for horses, ostriches, oxen, locusts, eagles, and hawks to achieve their created purpose in the world. By implication, if he so cares for the animals, how much more does he care for Job?

So, while the divine speeches make Job's finitude clear, their focus is on Yahweh's power and wisdom in creating and ruling his world. God rebukes Job, along with the other characters and the audience; calling him, and us, to a new wisdom of trust and even wonder—a discipline of humility and a faith in God's ability to rule his world justly and lovingly, even in the midst of mystery and reoccurring suffering.

As we noted above, in 42:3 Job returns to God's opening question from 38:2 and acknowledges that he has indeed obscured God's counsel without knowledge. He spoke of things he did not understand, things too wonderful for him to know. Job's encounter with God has moved him to a different place; he has received no answer as to why he suffered, but resolution has come through his existential encounter with God. Job has come face to face with the limits of his knowledge and has submitted to the mystery of God's purposes.

> Job has come face to face with the limits of his knowledge and has submitted to the mystery of God's purposes.

Human autonomy and a strong sense of "our truth" often manifests itself in a bucket approach to knowledge,[11] where we try to scoop up endless facts and arrange them logically. Job's growth in wisdom here is better understood in terms of the torchlight approach; what we see and know is always in relation to the light shone on the situation. Through his encounter with God, Job's torchlight has been cracked wide open and expanded so as to bring a new perspective on life. Somehow, in God's immense and wonderful design, injustice is allowed to play a role in God making things right again, or even better than they were before. *Job does not know how*, but spiritually he is in a position to accept that God can make even this situation work for his good purposes.

Job's last words—"Therefore I despise myself and repent in dust and ashes" (42:6)—create even more debate. On the surface, it seems as though Job is repenting, but the Hebrew is ambiguous. In the first phrase, the Hebrew verb *m's* could mean "refuse," "reject," or even "loathe," as many translations render the verb in Job's other use of this phrase in 9:21.[12] However, regardless of translation, it is not entirely clear what Job means. The second phrase is equally troubling. Habel translates it "I leave my ashes," which alerts us to the significance of the word "ashes" in this context. F. I. Anderson and others relate this clause to the "dust and ashes" that Abraham speaks of in Genesis 18:27. Here dust and ashes allude to our created nature— our humanity.[13] We are, after all, just animated earth or breathing clay. Adam and Eve were made from the dust (Gen 2:7) and were destined to return to dust upon their death (Gen 3:19). If Job has these contexts in mind, this verse brings us to a summary statement for the book: Humans are gifted with wisdom, but it is, nevertheless, the wisdom of *creatures*—of animated dust—and not of the infinite divine. In a world of suffering, we are profoundly limited in our understanding and lament our fallen and distorted creatureliness.

**SUGGESTED READING**

☐   Job 38–42

## Reflection

How would you describe the development in Job's understanding of God?

_____

_____

_____

J. B. Phillips wrote a book titled *Your God Is Too Small*. Do you think this was true of Job?

_____

_____

_____

Are there ways in which this is true of you?

_____

_____

_____

Have you ever been through a difficult time that has enlarged your view of God?

_____

_____

_____

# THE POWER
# OF POETRY

One of the fascinating characteristics of Job is that the bulk of the book, chapters 3–41, are written in poetry. This section is enclosed by the frame of 1–2 and 42, which are written in narrative prose. This makes it unlikely that Job should be read as a historical account, although there is debate about this among scholars. What is crucial is that we not make the false distinction that "historical" means the same thing as "true" and "fictional" means "false." Literature can be true and powerfully convey truth without being historical in the sense of recounting events that actually happened. For example, I grew up in apartheid South Africa, and to this day when I speak publicly about South Africa I always turn to Alan Paton's classic novel, *Cry, the Beloved Country*. Although Paton's book is a novel and thus the characters and plot are not strictly historical, the book powerfully evokes the relational breakdown that occurred in apartheid South Africa, with its racism and oppression. Story and poetry are able to evoke human experience in a way that straightforward descriptions cannot.

We know this well from the Psalms. It is one thing to say: "God is loving and he cares for his people." It is far more evocative and rich to say with Psalm 23, "The LORD is my shepherd, I shall not want ..." Job is narrative art at its best, and it is significant that most of Job is in *poetry*. Poetry is uniquely suited to plumb the depths of Job's

> Poetry is uniquely suited to plumb the depths of Job's suffering, to evoke his tragedy, to alert us to the sterility of the friends' speeches, and to set God before us as the majestic creator and sovereign of the universe.

suffering, to evoke his tragedy, to alert us to the sterility of the friends' speeches, and to set God before us as the majestic creator and sovereign of the universe. The friends' speeches, like the Psalter, resort to stereotypical images but lack the life of the Psalms. "Eliphaz," says Alter, "speaks smugly without suspecting that there might be a chasm between divine knowledge and the conventional knowledge of accepted wisdom."[1] Elihu's poetry is more powerful and sophisticated than the friends', though it does not, as Alter says, "soar like the Voice from the Whirlwind"[2] in chapters 38–41. Job is not afraid to protest, and Alter notes, "Job's cosmic poetry, unlike that of the friends, has a certain energy of vision, as though it proceeded from some immediate perception of the great things it reports."[3]

## PARALLELISM IN HEBREW POETRY

There are at least three types of parallelism in Hebrew poetry. In synonymous parallelism, the second line restates or supports the idea of the first line (Job 3:11). In antithetic parallelism, the second line contrasts the idea of the first line (Job 8:7). Finally, in developmental (or synthetic) parallelism, the second line expands or builds on the idea of the first line (Job 5:19).

The great characteristic of Hebrew poetry is that of parallelism, in which one or more lines work in parallel with the first line.[4] Even if you cannot read Hebrew, this characteristic is evident from the way modern versions set out poetry in their translations. It is rare for Hebrew poetry simply to repeat the same thought in a second or third line; normally there is an intensification of some sort or the development of the idea in some way. Take Job 38:2, for example, which we can set out as follows:

> Who is this
> that darkens my counsel
> with words without knowledge?

The phrase "with words without knowledge" parallels "that darkens my counsel." But it more than reproduces the idea, it intensifies it by showing how Job darkens God's counsel, namely by speaking without true knowledge. In the Hebrew there is also a play on letters in "words without": Both words contain the Hebrew letters *b*, *l*, and *y*, thereby highlighting the emptiness of the words.

Many other features of Hebrew poetry are similar to those of modern poetry, including evocative
language, allusion, the use of metaphors and similes,
plays on words, etc. In 38:2 above, for example, God
speaks of one who "darkens" his counsel. In the Old
Testament, "counsel" is associated with wisdom and
light, but here we are alerted to a form of speech that
casts a shadow over God's wisdom.[5] Like good poetry,
it leads us to ponder this image and ask a host of questions such as how, why, in what way, etc. Such an image would also have cut Job to the heart. He had longed
for God to appear and to be held accountable, and now
he stands accused of darkening God's counsel!

Job's speeches are a rich repository of poetry and
readers are encouraged to explore them in this way.
Let's look more closely at Job's final words before
Elihu's speech and then God's speeches. Job 31:35–40
lead up to the narrator's note in 31:40—"The words
of Job are ended." This statement is itself significant,
indicating that Job really has nothing more to say; he
has run out of words. Job 31:35–40 reads as follows:

> ("Oh, that I had someone to hear me!
>   I sign now my defense—let the Almighty an-
> swer me;
>   let my accuser put his indictment in writing.
> Surely I would wear it on my shoulder,
>   I would put it on like a crown.
> I would give him an account of my every step;
>   I would present it to him as to a ruler.)—
>
> "if my land cries out against me
>   and all its furrows are wet with tears,
> if I have devoured its yield without payment

> or broken the spirit of its tenants,
> then let briers come up instead of wheat
> and stinkweed instead of barley."

The words of Job are ended.

In 31:35 Job first expresses his great desire to be heard, and especially by God. In his speeches, Job often expresses the desire to take God to court so that God will be forced to explain himself. Here again in 31:35 we have the language of a law court, indicated by the Hebrew word for "indictment," which refers to a legal case against, in this case, Job.

The lines, "Let the Almighty answer me; let my accuser put his indictment in writing," are parallel—the second line intensifying the meaning of the first. Job requires not just an answer but a legal indictment explaining the case against him in writing. The Almighty is also identified in the second line as Job's accuser. Job signing off on his case also anticipates "The words of Job are ended" in 31:40. Job knows that his case is hopeless: How can he get the Almighty to submit his case in writing? But he has had enough and has nothing more to say. Going to court is often our last desperate measure for justice, and Job here, as it were, reviews his case, is satisfied with it, and signs off on it. There is absolutely nothing more he feels he can do.

The parallelism in 31:36–7 is easily identifiable:

> Surely I would wear it on my shoulder,
> I would put it on like a crown.
> I would give him an account of my every step;
> I would present it to him as to a ruler.

The second line in 31:36 intensifies the thought of the first. Job imagines God's written indictment as something he would want everyone to see; it would virtually establish him as royalty—"like a crown"—because, in Job's mind, it would establish his innocence.

In 31:37 the second line develops the first. In the first line, Job states that he will provide God with an exhaustive report of his life. In the second line, he says he will present it to God with humility and reverence as befits a ruler. Job again pleads his innocence in 31:38–40, this time with the central metaphor of the land. This concern for the land and its inhabitants anticipates God's concern for the whole creation. Indeed, the book of Job contains major resources for an environmental ethic. Job knows that God loves the creation, the land, and its peoples, and in these verses he personifies the land, similar to the way the Lord does in Genesis 4:10—where God speaks of the land as crying out over the spilling of Abel's blood. Job knows that humans have a responsibility to care for and steward the land. And as a great landowner, he speaks of "my land" in Job 31:38.

In Genesis 4 the land cries out against Cain, and here Job says that if he has caused the land to cry out and its furrows to weep through abuse and evil, and if he has practiced economic exploitation of its inhabitants (31:39), then God should be free to curse the land (31:40) as he did with Adam and Eve. The same Hebrew words are used here for "cry out" and "land" as in Genesis 4:11, but the words for "briers" and "stinkweed" differ from the words in Genesis 3:18, though the idea is the same. The implication is, of course, that Job is innocent of any such crimes and undeserving of

the suffering he is going through. If he has the early
chapters of Genesis in mind, then his plea is that even
if he is guilty—which he is sure he is not—then let the
punishment fit the crime as with Adam and Eve, and
Cain, but not this unbearable and disproportionate
hell he is going through.

This short section of Job's concluding words gives
us a taste of the power of poetry to evoke Job's pain
and desperation. Thus, first, poetry enables the book
of Job to evoke the depth of the tragedy that struck Job.
The Jewish thinker George Steiner argues, using Job
as an example, that "Tragedy is alien to the Judaic
[Jewish] sense of the
world";[6] tragedy in his
view is essentially an
ancient Greek affair
and arises from a view
of the world in which

> Poetry enables the book of
> Job to evoke the depth of
> the tragedy that struck Job.

humans encounter blind necessity. C. S. Lewis once
commented that his greatest fear was not that there
was no God, but that God was not good. The Greeks
struggled with something even worse. They had no
view of a personal, good God governing the world and
thought that ultimately they were at the mercy of an
impersonal force who governed their lives without
any concern for their well-being and whose control
was inescapable!

Clearly what Job encounters is not blind necessity but the difficulty of squaring his suffering with
the God he serves. Job's struggle is closer to C. S.
Lewis' fear. Steiner's definition of tragedy is, however, narrow, and it remains valuable to see Job in
the context of the struggle with tragedy in ancient

and modern literature. The American philosopher Martha Nussbaum notes the important role of narrative and image in learning about morality: "Certain truths about human experience can best be learned by living them in their particularity. Nor can this particularity be grasped solely by thought 'itself for itself.' "[7] This relates to her point that a contribution of tragedy is to explore the gap between what we are and how well we manage to live our lives.[8] The book of Job, with its poetry and vivid and sterile images, evokes precisely such tragic particularity. As Henri Nouwen noted, often the most personal is the most universal. By allowing us to see the gap between Job at his lowest—amid the direst circumstances—and his eventual restoration and development, the poetry of Job enables us to look again at our struggles and to find hope for where God may be at work in them.

Unlike his opponents who held to an abstract view of virtue, the ancient Greek philosopher Aristotle saw the emotions of pity and fear as central to tragedy and valuable as sources of illumination and clarification.[9] Job is full of the range of emotions and the book expects his readers to be formed as they journey with Job through his tragedy to resolution.

The Christian theologian Peter Leithart refers to the Christian perspective on life as one of "deep comedy." He is, of course, using "comedy" in an unusual sense to refer to the fact that the ending the Bible envisages is uncontaminated by any fear of future tragedy, and the characters progress to a fulfillment that exceeds their beginning; the move is from glory to glory. However, as Leithart rightly notes, such deep comedy does not erase tragedy; it simply enables us to see it in all its painful depths as "deep tragedy."

> Because the resurrection vindicates the Crucified, not the crucifixion, the gospel story undercuts any easy moralism or sentimental liberalism. ... Thus the cross and resurrection intensify sadness and the sense of loss, and in a sense make tragedy more tragic.[10]

As Plantinga notes, "There could be no such thing as genuinely horrifying evil if there were no God."[11] There is thus a sense in which Bernard Williams is right to criticize moral philosophy's attachment to serving up "good news" about our condition.[12] A role of tragedy, and not least that of Job, is to confront us with the horrors inherent in fallen human life. The critical difference, of course, between Job and Greek tragedy with its horrifying blind necessity, is the central character of Job, God, and God's providential ordering of his good creation.

> A role of tragedy, and not least that of Job, is to confront us with the horrors inherent in fallen human life.

Poetry also enables us to catch a vision of God as creator and sovereign over his universe. The divine speeches in Job are remarkable:

> If the poetry of Job ... looms above all other biblical poetry in virtuosity and sheer expressive power, the culminating poem that God speaks out of the storm soars beyond

everything that has preceded it in the book,
the poet having wrought a poetic idiom
even richer and more awesome than the
one he gave Job.[13]

When God finally answers Job out of the
whirlwind, he responds with an order of
poetry formally allied to Job's own remarkable poetry, but larger in scope and greater
in power... That is, God picks up many of
Job's key images, especially from the death-
wish poem with which Job began (Chapter
3) and his discourse is shaped by a powerful movement of intensification, coupled
with an implicitly narrative sweep from the
creation to the play of natural forces to the
teeming world of animal life.[14]

Scholars debate whether the divine speeches
are an answer to Job's experience of suffering.[15]
C. A. Newsom discerns a multiplicity of voices in Job
and argues that no voice, not even God's, provides an
answer to the questions raised in the book. In his review of Newsom's *The Book of Job: A Contest of Moral
Imaginations*, Jon Levenson perceptively notes, "Three
centuries of secularization and historical criticism
impel us to place God's words about himself on a plane
with human speculations about him. There is ample
reason to doubt that ancient Israelites felt the same
agnostic impulse or evaluated interminable dialogue
with no chance of resolution so highly."[16]

It is true that Job receives no direct answer as to
why he suffered. But Job confesses that he had previ-
ously only *heard* of God but now he *sees* him, which

tells us that his suffering has worked a profound transformation in him. The divine speeches answer Job but not the questions *he* was asking. The repetition of the reference to darkening counsel in 38:2 and 42:3 that frame God's speeches—in biblical studies we refer to this enveloped structure as an *inclusio*—and Job's reference back to 38:2 in

> Job confesses that he had previously only *heard* of God but now he *sees* him, which tells us that his suffering has worked a profound transformation in him.

42:3 indicate that God's speeches have indeed achieved their aim. God's agenda is radically different to Job's and the divine speeches facilitate the momentous shift in Job from knowing about God to deep, interpersonal relationship in which Job assumes and embraces his creaturely status.

A surprising aspect of the divine speeches is their focus on the non-human aspects of the creation. Kathryn Schifferdecker rightly mentions this non-human emphasis but falsely, in my view, concludes that the divine speeches are unique in the Bible in this respect. Creation, and *not covenant*, she stresses, is where Job's answer is to be found. However, the recurrence of *Yahweh*, the great covenantal name of Israel's God (see also Exod 3; 6) in Job 42, plus the reference to a burnt offering (Job 42:8), undercut any non-covenantal reading. And in terms of the unique place of humankind in the creation, we should remember that it is Job who is taken on the tour of creation, not an ostrich or a donkey![17]

The divine speeches do not articulate a different creation theology to what is portrayed in the rest of the Old Testament. But they place the emphasis on the non-human in order to facilitate the decentering of Job—a part of his transformation process. Job needs to realize that there is far more to the creation than him, and the focus on nature and animals intentionally broadens his perspective that has—understandably—become obsessed with *his own* experience. In Job 3, Job's attempt to un-create the world is centered around himself; the divine speeches focus on Yahweh and the world *apart from* Job and humankind.

Rolf P. Knierim perceptively notes:

> Job is told that his challenge to Yahweh's justice is evaluated on the basis of the universal order of Yahweh's created and sustained world and not on the basis of his own experience. To the extent that Job saw Yahweh withdrawing from the wholeness of his life he was correct. But he was wrong when challenging Yahweh's justice universally. For such a challenge, his experience was not universal enough. His experience cannot be the sum total of wisdom because it does not represent the structure of the whole world, just as he himself is not the creator and sustainer of this structure.[18]

God's speeches are truly remarkable. George Steiner commented that on a good day he can imagine the great Shakespeare sitting at home and writing his plays, but he cannot imagine any human writing these speeches of God in Job. There really is something divine about them. The novelist Frederick Buechner says of God's speeches:

> Just the way God cleared his throat almost blasted Job off his feet, and that was only for starters. It is the most gorgeous speech that God makes in the whole Old Testament, and it is composed almost entirely of the most gorgeous and preposterous questions that have ever been asked by God or anybody else.[19]

In 38:2–38 God focuses poetically on his work of and in creation, and then in 38:39–30 he moves on to the animals of creation. In 40:6–14 God speaks of his justice, a theme much closer to home for Job, and then in 40:15–41:34 he discusses the Behemoth and the Leviathan—great and mysterious creatures that humankind cannot control, but God can.

We have already noted how questions dominate God's speeches. My psychologist friend encourages me in difficult meetings to *ask questions*, as it makes the other party do the work on the issues under discussion. This is precisely what God's questions are designed to do—to make Job reflect hard on *who he is* in relation to Yahweh.

God's speeches are full of rich metaphors, allusions, and evocative expressions, all designed to bring home to Job the reality of the expanse of creation and God's powerful, caring rule of the whole. As we saw above in our exploration of Job's final words, Job pleads, "Let the Almighty answer me" (31:35). Whereas here in 38:3 the Lord says to Job, "I will question you, and you shall answer me."

A series of evocative questions appear in 38:4–38, showing Job that Yahweh is the creator and he is a creature. Their poetic form allows the questions to be posed with great force and energy. Take a moment to read Genesis 1:1–2:3 and then this section of Job. Both describe creation, but it is immediately apparent that Job 38 is poetry whereas Genesis 1 is narrative prose. You do not find in Genesis 1 references to the sea bursting forth from the womb (38:8), to God making the clouds the garment in which he wraps the sea (38:9) or the "proud waves" (38:11), to giving orders to the morning and showing the dawn its place (38:12), to the storehouses of the snow and hail (38:22), to the road to the place where lightning is dispersed (38:24), etc. This is rhetoric of a high order all designed to show, as God's ironic question in 38:21 demonstrates, "Surely you know, for you were already born! You have lived so many years!"—that Job is a creature with a limited time span, with a limited perspective, and thus with limited knowledge.

In Job 38:39–40 and in 40:15–41:34 God draws Job's attention to the animal world. God created humankind in his own image, to be God's royal steward to care for and develop the creation in a way that images the great king over all the creation (Gen 1:26–28). Therefore, God cares about the animal world, as should humans, and is depicted in these chapters as being in direct relationship with that world. For example, in Job 38:41, the young ravens cry out *to God* for food in a time of famine. God's questions to Job demonstrate what Job doesn't know or do, but, at the same time, they indicate what God *does* know and do! Job 39:1–2, for example, implies that God does take an interest in and knows when the mountain goats give birth. It is God who grants the wild donkey freedom (39:5–8) and a place to thrive and hills to range for forage. Job 39:7 personifies the donkey as laughing at the commotion in the town and ignoring the shout of a driver. These verses point out that there is life apart from humans in the creation, which implies that there is far more to life than Job. We get the sense that God takes delight in these non-human aspects of his creation and is genuinely concerned that his creations thrive and flourish. For example, in 39:13–18 there is humor in the stupidity of the ostrich in her dealings with her young but admiration in the speed at which she can run.

> God takes delight in these non-human aspects of his creation and is genuinely concerned that his creations thrive and flourish.

God's questions to Job about nature and the animal world all relate to the immense difference between Job as a person and God as the omnipotent creator. In 40:7–14 this difference is related specifically to Job's questioning of God's justice. Remember, Job did not get to see the heaven scenes in Job 1–2, as we did, and God doesn't explain to Job why he was subjected to such suffering. Instead, God draws Job's attention to *his* greatness and Job's smallness by comparison. This leads on to the discussion of the Behemoth and the Leviathan (40:15–41:34) as examples of creatures that humankind cannot control but which God knows and is sovereign over. Buechner rightly notes:

He [Job] had seen the great glory so shot
through with sheer, fierce light and gladness, had heard the great voice raised in
song so full of terror and wildness and
beauty, that from that moment on, nothing
else mattered. All possible questions melted like mist, and all possible explanations
withered like grass, and all the bad times
of his life together with all the good times
were so caught up into the fathomless life of
this God, who had bent down to speak with
him though by comparison he was no more
than a fleck of dust on the head of a pin in
the lapel of a dancing flea, that all he could
say was, "I had heard of thee by the hearing,
but now my eyes see thee: therefore I despise myself and repent in dust and ashes"
(Job 42:5–6).[20]

## SUGGESTED READING

- ☐   Genesis 1–3
- ☐   Job 29–31

## Reflection

Take a short section from Job 29–31. Does reading it
closely and attentively as poetry help you to empa-
thize with Job's suffering? How so?

_____

_____

Can you think of a novel or poem that has had a profound effect on your life?

_____

_____

_____

Why do you think it was a poem or novel that affected you in this way?

_____

_____

_____

How is the literary form of Job as a story with poetry peculiarly suited to deal with the subject of unexpected and terrible suffering?

_____

_____

_____

# JOB'S JOURNEY OF TRANSFORMATION

A reading of Job as a story containing long stretches of poetry alerts us to its central theme of *formation through suffering*. It is very useful to examine some books of the Bible through the lens of another discipline. For example, Ellen Davis, in *Scripture, Culture, and Agriculture*,[1] opens up a fruitful dialogue between the Old Testament and the new agrarianism, and with Wendell Berry in particular; the results are very insightful.

With Job, psychology is such a discipline. An experience like Job's is ripe for psychological analysis, and in this section we will use insights from Jung to explore Job's experience.[2] Susannah Ticciati rightly notes that *the self* and its being transformed are central to Job.[3] Within the Jungian tradition Edward F. Edinger proposes a more helpful reading of Job than Jung himself, according to which Job recounts a comprehensive account of the encounter with the Self.[4]

## JUNG ON JOB

The eminent psychologist Carl Jung's fullest treat-
ment of the book of Job can be found in his 1952
book *Antwort auf Hiob* (translated into English in
1954 as *Answer to Job*). In it, Jung controversially
proposes that God did wrong by allowing the righteous Job to be afflicted.

For Jung, the Self is the center of the total person,
conscious and unconscious, whereas the Ego is the
center of conscious personality. Further, the Ego is
the center of subjective identity while the Self is the
locale of objective identity. The Self is identified by
Jung with the *imago dei*; it is the creative center where
God and humankind meet—what Old Testament wisdom calls "the heart."

Psychologically, the relationship between the Ego
and the Self is vitally important. Many psychological problems are illuminated in terms of the Ego-Self
relationship. Jung distinguishes between the inflated
Ego, the alienated Ego, and the Ego's encounter with
the Self, leading to a healthy relationship between the
Ego and the Self. Inflation refers to the identification
of the Ego with the Self. "It is a state in which something small (the Ego) has arrogated to itself the quali-
ties of something larger (the Self) and hence is blown
up beyond the limits of its proper size."[5] However, this
state cannot continue indefinitely because the experience of life frustrates the expectations of the inflated
Ego, resulting in an estrangement between the Ego
and the Self. "This estrangement is symbolized by
such images as a fall, an exile, an unhealing wound,

a perpetual torture."[6] This experience of alienation is, from this perspective, a necessary stage en route to awareness of and a healthy relationship to the self.

According to Jung, "The self, in its efforts at self-realization, reaches out beyond the ego-personality on all sides; because of its all-encompassing nature it is brighter and darker than the ego, and accordingly confronts it with problems which it would like to avoid. ... For this reason, the experience of the self is always a defeat for the ego."[7] The inflation of the ego is thus symptomatic of the idolatry of the "I" as the center of one's existence, rather than the "I" finding its identity in relation to God. The journey toward health involves a decentering of the ego, the "I," as *part of* the self and as *constituted by* the self, but not *as* the self. For Søren Kierkegaard, the 19th-century Danish Christian philosopher, as for Jung, the process of moving from an inflated Ego, through an alienated Ego, to a healthy Ego-Self relationship is wrought by pain and struggle—for it is a journey that the Ego instinctively resists.[8] Maturity or inner transformation is thus nothing less than an encounter with the Self.

How does this theory help us understand what Job undergoes? When Job loses everything he holds valuable, he is plunged into despair and a state of alienation. If the Self, from a Jungian perspective, is to be recognized as the supreme value, then all lesser attachments—those most closely connected with the inflation of the Ego—*must*

> He needed to grow and develop as a believer, to advance in what we call sanctification— becoming holy, becoming like God, becoming whole.

*be loosened*. This is not to suggest that Job was not a true believer, but it is to argue that he needed to grow and develop as a believer, to advance in what we call *sanctification*—becoming holy, becoming like God, becoming whole.

Job evidently centered the meaning of his life in family, property, and health. The indications of this are found in his obsessive protection of his family in 1:5 and in his inflated vision of what should happen to him at death in 3:14–15 (see also 30:1), where he imagines himself at peace with the great and wise ones of the earth! When deprived of his attachments, he despaired and entered what St. John of the Cross calls the "dark night of the soul."[9] Job's life has shattered and his response is to seek to cause creation to shatter (Job 3).[10] Alter describes Job 3 as "a powerful, evocative, authentic expression of man's essential, virtually ineluctable egotism."[11] Schifferdecker adds, "Job's own world has descended into turmoil or chaos (ζγρ), and he attempts to inflict that chaos on creation itself; first by cursing creation, then by ascribing chaotic tendencies to God."[12] Job remains convinced of his innocence and for Edinger, he thereby demonstrates that he is unconscious of the dark, "shadow side" of his personality. The repetitiveness of the dialogues, which so irritate the impatient reader, enact this performatively in the reading process, since the resistance of the ego involves returning again and again and again to the same issues. The friends, incidentally, similarly show that they are unaware of the shadow sides of their personalities since they, too, return again and again and again to the same issues.

From Edinger's perspective, the centrality of God in Job is deeply significant since it provides the assurance that there is meaning in Job's suffering. Through his encounters with God, Job is brought to the realization that the Ego is ignorant of the Self in its totality, or, as we might say, of his creatureliness. He is not God. Satan's suggestion that Job will curse God, and the encouragement to do so by his wife, highlight the issue of Ego inflation. "Therefore the program is arranged to test the ego in the fire of tribulation, and out of that ordeal comes Job's full encounter with the reality of God. ... we can say that it was God's purpose to make Job aware of Him."[13] Through his riveting encounter with God, "Job's questions have been answered, not rationally but by living experience. What he has been seeking, the meaning of his suffering, has been found. It is nothing less than the conscious realization of the autonomous archetypal psyche; and this realization could come to birth *only through an ordeal*."[14]

This may seem like a lot of complicated theory for a rather simple solution: Job has to realize that he is a creature and not God. And it's easy to think, "We are Christians, we know that already!" But as Job had to learn, there is a difference between knowing about something, and *knowing* it in the depths of one's heart. The quest for human autonomy—for humans to be a law unto themselves rather than to have to submit to God's ways—is the sin that introduced sin into the world in Genesis 3. And this quest echoes down through history in a myriad of ways and is arguably *the sin* of the modern world. Modernity, with all its many good things, is deeply founded on a desire to do without God and to place humankind at the center of life. This toxin is in our wiring and it is *not* easily dismissed.

Yes, the truth of Job is ultimately simple, but it is also profound. Job arrives at what Proverbs calls the starting point, namely: "The fear of the LORD is the beginning of wisdom" (Prov 1:7; 9:10). But it is not a starting point we ever leave behind. Rather, as the great poet T. S. Eliot might remind us, it is a starting point that we return to again and again, to see and understand it more fully:

> We shall not cease from exploration
> And the end of all our exploring
> Will be to arrive where we started
> And know the place for the first time.[15]

Wisdom is not just head knowledge, but an existential knowledge of God that needs to permeate and reform our entire being. Job reminds us that this will often be a traumatic process. It will mean, from time to time, going through the furnace of formation.

A literary and psychological reading illumines the fact that the book of Job, like Ecclesiastes, is about the transformative dimension essential to true wisdom. "The Book of Job is really a record of a divine initiation process, a testing by ordeal, which when successful, leads to a new state of being."[16]

A literary and psychological reading illumines the fact that the book of Job, like Ecclesiastes, is about the transformative dimension essential to true wisdom.

**SUGGESTED READING**

☐ If you are interested in a psychological reading of Job and can get hold of Edward F. Edinger's *Ego and Archetype* (Baltimore: Penguin, 1972), you might like to read Edinger's section on Job, pp.76–96.

☐ For a comparable reading of Ecclesiastes, see Craig G. Bartholomew, *Ecclesiastes.* BCOTWP. (Grand Rapids: Baker, 2009), 375–89.

☐ The Bible is full of stories of formation through trials. Read Jonah, for example, and compare his journey with Job's.

## Reflection

Do you find a psychological reading of Job helpful? Why or why not?

_____

_____

_____

What does Job's journey teach you about what to look for in a good counselor?

_____

_____

_____

Does Job's journey of transformation cast light on any hard times you have been through?

_____

_____

_____

# 7

# JOB AND JESUS

The only mention of Job in the New Testament is found in James 5:11:

> As you know, we count as blessed those who have persevered. You have heard of Job's perseverance and have seen what the Lord finally brought about. The Lord is full of compassion and mercy.

James was Jesus' brother and we would be wise to pay close attention to his letter. James has much to say about trials and temptations, and his reference to Job comes in a section dealing with patience and perseverance in suffering (Jas 5:7–12). His two examples of perseverance amid suffering are the prophets and Job. He perceptively refers to "what the Lord has finally brought about" in Job and follows this with an astonishing statement, "The Lord is full of compassion and mercy." James' reference to perseverance in chapter 5 likely connects to his

> James rightly alerts us to Job's story as an example of perseverance in suffering and of God's formative work through that suffering.

discussion of perseverance in chapter 1, in which he notes that perseverance is vital for God's formative work to take place. Thus James rightly alerts us to Job's story as an example of perseverance in suffering and of God's formative work through that suffering.

## JOB ELSEWHERE IN THE BIBLE

Besides Job and James, the only other biblical book to mention Job is Ezekiel. In Ezekiel 14:14, 20, Job is mentioned alongside Noah and Daniel as positive examples whose righteousness cannot be transferred to anyone else.

In Job 28:12, Job asks, "Where can wisdom be found?" The New Testament unequivocally answers, "In Christ." The most extensive christological reading of Job in modern times is that by the German theologian Karl Barth, who devotes 100 pages to Job.[1] Barth argues that Job is a type of Christ as the true witness and his encounter with the falsehood of humanity. The New Testament does not identify Job as a major source for understanding Jesus, but in the context of Jesus as wisdom personified it is surely legitimate to make this connection. As with Job, suffering is central to the wisdom of Jesus. Hebrews 5:8-9 points out that, like Job, suffering was transformative for Jesus; through it he learned obedience and became perfect. Jesus' suffering, like Job's, is hellish; at the Mount of Olives he is in anguish, and his sweat is like great drops of blood (Luke 22:39-46).

Unlike Job, Jesus does not protest the injustice of God except in the very darkest moments of the garden of Gethsemane and from the cross ("My God, my God, why have you forsaken me?"). Unlike Job, Jesus, in his suffering, takes upon himself the burden of the world's guilt and sin. Unlike Job, Jesus dies, crushed by that burden, but rises triumphantly to open the gates of the kingdom to all. Central to the biblical narrative is the slain Lamb upon the throne; his death will ultimately remove all suffering. But in the time between his inauguration of the kingdom and its consummation, believers will continue to suffer and continue to need a book like Job. Yet, we know that our Redeemer lives and that we shall live to see him.

> Christians need to be prepared to suffer like Jesus, and therefore we can look to Job as a vital resource for discipleship.

In the Gospels, Jesus exhorts us to take up our cross and follow him (Matt 10:38; 16:24; Mark 8:34; Luke 9:23). He identifies this as an indispensable mark of being one of his followers. As one commentator perceptively notes, in the ancient world, if you were to take up a cross, there was only one destination in view: crucifixion. Thus, Christians need to be prepared to suffer like Jesus, and therefore we can look to Job as a vital resource for discipleship.

## SUGGESTED READING

☐  Mark 8:27–9:1

☐  Hebrews 5:1–9

## Reflection

In what ways is Job similar and different to Jesus?

_____

_____

_____

Now that Jesus has come, why do we still need a book like Job?

_____

_____

_____

# 8

# THE READER'S JOURNEY OF TRANSFORMATION

What then should we learn from the extraordinary book of Job? First, we should read it as the immensely practical book it is. Some biblical scholarship has been unhelpful in this respect, doing everything with Job apart from reading it to hear God's transformative word. In his *Repetition*, Søren Kierkegaard provides a far healthier example of how to live with Job:

> If I did not have Job! It is impossible to describe all the shades of meaning and how manifold the meaning is that he has for me. I do not read him as one reads another book, with the eyes, but I lay the book, as it were, on my heart and read it with the eyes of the heart, in a clairvoyance, interpreting the specifics in the most diverse ways. Just as the child puts his schoolbook under his pillow to make sure he has not forgotten his lesson when he wakes up in the morning, so I take the book to bed with me at night. Every word by him is food and clothing and

healing for my wretched soul. Now a word by him arouses me from my lethargy and awakens new restlessness; now it calms the sterile raging within me, stops the dreadfulness in the mute nausea of my passion. Have you really read Job? ... Every transcription of this kind is laid upon my sick heart as God's hand-plaster. ... Nowhere in the world has the passion of anguish found such expression. ... At night I can have all the lights burning, the whole house illuminated. Then I stand up and read in a loud voice, almost shouting, some passage from him. ... Although I have read the book again and again, each word remains new to me. ... Like an inebriate, I imbibe all the intoxication of passion little by little, until by this prolonged sipping I become almost unconscious in drunkenness.[1]

Kierkegaard was not unfamiliar with suffering, and he rightly saw the need to read Job so that it penetrated to the core of his being. We should do likewise.

### KIERKEGAARD AND JOB

The Danish philosopher Søren Kierkegaard wrote on the book of Job twice, both in 1843: first as part of his book *Repetition*, and second in his "edifying discourse" on Job 1:20–21, "The Lord Gave, and the Lord Hath Taken Away, Blessed Be the Name of the Lord."

Second, we should learn from Job that suffering can be part of our discipleship. We should never go looking for suffering; this was a mistake that some Christians in the early church made, thinking that martyrdom was the highest act of service. If we can avoid suffering, we should. But it is rare for a person to avoid it their entire life. Suffering has a way of finding us when it needs to, as it did with Job.

There are many reasons why people suffer. Sometimes *it is* because of our sin; sin can, and does, cause suffering. Think of a murderer sitting in prison. Prison is no fun, but he or she has brought such suffering upon her or himself. Substance abuse is another example. Such abuse of the body is sinful and can result in horrible addiction. But often suffering is not because of sin—contrary to what some parts of the health, wealth, and prosperity movement would have us believe. Christians, especially in North America, are often tempted to believe that suffering is always the result of (personal) sin and that if we only obey God, then prosperity will result.

But by no means is all suffering related to sin. Bad things do happen to good people and Job is *the* Old Testament reminder of that truth. The lengthy speeches of Job's friends further remind us how debilitating and shameful a simplistic application of the sin-equals-suffering connection can be. Indeed, the counsel of Job's friends is itself condemned by God as sinful (see 42:7). Job's story also shows us that sometimes the godliest people are called to live through terrible suffering, and it is quite evil to tell such people that their suffering is because of their sin, as Bildad did to Job (8:4).

Some Christians, even if they don't believe that all suffering results from sin, have an unhealthy habit of sidelining people when they go through messy and protracted experiences, rather than recognizing that God may be deeply at work in the mess, uncovering amazing gifts in the process. We need to recover *a Christianity of the cross*, recognizing that just as our Lord suffered, so, too, may we. And if we wait with such suffering, we might be surprised what the Lord has wrought through it.

> Just as our Lord suffered, so, too, may we. And if we wait with such suffering, we might be surprised what the Lord has wrought through it.

Third, we should recognize that God uses suffering to form his people at the deepest level. In this respect, we can use the book of Job to identify many characteristics of suffering.

It is no accident that Job deals with suffering through the *story* of an individual. In practice, suffering is never something in the abstract, like a philosophical argument; rather it is rooted in the life—the story—of a particular person. It is deeply existential, and to understand it we need to know the story of the person involved. We have seen how Job's story gives us clues as to what God might be doing—and will continue to do—through suffering.

But what is the nature of suffering? Nouwen rightly notes that *our own wounds* are the hardest to carry through to healing. It is one thing to be there for others when they suffer; it is quite another to live through our own, deep suffering. The thing about suffering is that it is horribly individual. It is *Job* who is going through his particular hell and not his friends. As Job comments in 3:25: "What *I* feared has come upon me; what *I* dreaded has happened to me." Deep suffering of Job's sort is unique and individual. If we compare Job with other characters in the Bible who suffer greatly, we will see how different suffering is for different individuals. Qohelet, the main character in Ecclesiastes—generally translated as "the Preacher"—suffers immensely, but he experiences more of an intellectual crisis that guts him to the core of his being as he desperately searches for meaning in life. Jonah also suffers, but in a very different way than Job and Qohelet. Deep suffering seems to shut us up into ourselves, since we alone are going through this horrendous experience. In *Les Miserables*, a character sings, "There is a grief that can't be spoken," which evokes the terrible individuality of deep suffering.

If suffering were expected, it would be much easier to deal with. We could prepare for it, read up about it, make sure we had the right support structures in place, and so on. But the nature of suffering is that it comes as a terrible surprise. Nothing could have prepared Job for what happened. One day all was well and the next his life was turned upside down so that it would never be the same. Even when suffering approaches more slowly, its intensity and terror still come as a dreadful surprise.

Suffering is also a mystery. We see this again and again in Job's story, as he struggles to make sense of what has happened to him. There is a great mystery to suffering and even when resolution comes it does not necessarily explain what and why this happened to *me*. Suffering always confronts us with this mystery because, like Job, we feel so deeply that if we only knew *why* this had happened, we might be able to cope with it.

It is painful to see the level of Job's vulnerability in his speeches and interaction with his friends. His life has been shattered and this leaves him very vulnerable. Amid suffering, we experience a range of emotions, some we hardly knew existed. We may move, like Job, from faith to raging despair, to anger with our friends, to longing to never have been born, to railing against God, and so on. We keep returning to our suffering like an itchy sore that we can't leave alone. Suffering envelops our horizon and we face it at every turn.

The result is that suffering is incredibly messy. There is nothing nice and ordered about deep suffering. It takes out our feet from under us and we, like a drowning person, desperately try to find ways to cope and get things back under control. We are not pleasant to be with: Emotionally we are a mess; we can't focus on anything apart from our ordeal; and we lash out at those who don't understand us. Job's relationship with his wife is a mess; his relationship with God seems to have vanished into thin air; his friends turn out to be no help; and he has gone from being respected to being despised.

The nature of suffering is that we are not in control of it. Job was used to being in control and giving advice to others. Then his life spun completely out of control, and he had no idea what to do about it. Job 29:1–6 is deeply informative in this respect:

Job continued his discourse:
"How I long for the months gone by,
    for the days when God watched over me,
when his lamp shone on my head
    and by his light I walked through darkness!
Oh, for the days when I was in my prime,
    when God's intimate friendship blessed
my house,
when the Almighty was still with me
    and my children were around me,
when my path was drenched with cream
    and the rock poured out for me streams of
olive oil.

Job looks back on times of "intimate friendship" with God. Job was no nominal Christian, but had experience of God's blessing and consolation. This is not to say that his life had always been easy, but of those dark times Job says, "By his light I walked through darkness." Job had experiential acquaintance with Psalm 23. He had known the Lord as his shepherd in good times and bad.

But now Job experiences something completely different. During the worst crisis of his life, when his need is greatest, God seems completely absent! In St. John of the Cross' language, this is a classic case of the dark night of the soul, in which God is experienced as absent in the midst of a suffocating darkness. This sort of

In St. John of the Cross' language, this is a classic case of the dark night of the soul, in which God is experienced as absent in the midst of a suffocating darkness.

suffering is uncontrollable. We may have experienced a kind of suffering where God is deeply present and sustains us through it. But in Job's type of suffering there is no sense of God's consolation; the world seems to have gone mad and God seems to have become your enemy rather than your great friend.

And this type of suffering is protracted. The book of Job demonstrates this for us through the long, repetitive speeches. Are they endless? That is just how such suffering feels. Each day drags and you may be unsure how you'll make it through this day, let alone the next one. Any plans you had for the future are dashed as life closes in to the immediate horror.

Because suffering is unexpected and so disorienting, we often have no choice as to which friends and counselors we turn to. Job's friends were exemplary in taking time out for him and in spending seven days with him in silence, mourning and lamenting. But once the dialogues begin, the friends become reactive, quickly seeking to interpret Job's suffering through the grid of their mechanical theologies. Tragically, they thereby enhance his suffering—as well-meaning friends can easily do. Job rightly says to his friends: "You, however, smear me with lies; you are worthless physicians, all of you!" (13:4).

Job's friends turn out to be examples of how *not* to be a good friend to someone who is suffering deeply. They are also the sort of friend to avoid, if possible, while you are suffering and vulnerable. Beware of friends who quickly impose their own concerns and categories upon you while you are in pain. Job's friends should have listened far more, been content to be with Job in his pain, affirmed the mystery of what he was going through, and, like Job, cried out to God for help and understanding.

Our world is full of suffering, and good friends and counselors are a great treasure. One thing we can learn from Job is to work to become that sort of friend, as well as to cultivate such friends in our own lives. Wonderfully, evangelicals nowadays are recovering the ancient practice of spiritual direction, and a wise spiritual director can be an invaluable resource during times of suffering.[2] One thing a wise spiritual director will never do is to try to play God; rather, the wise director will accompany us on a journey of discerning and seeking God's ways.

We discussed above the value of a psychological reading of Job. Psychology and psychiatry are, at their best, great gifts and can be of great help in difficult times. Sadly, however, much psychology and psychiatry is thoroughly secular and deliberately does not take the living God into account. As Job found, ultimately it was God he needed, and resolution comes though an encounter with God. Deep suffering focuses on the question of whether God is for real. Even with all the help we can get—and we should seek help in suffering—there is no alternative to waiting for God and finding resolution in and through him.

One great lesson from Job is that we should be utterly real before God in the midst of suffering. We can rage, shout, protest, scream, and cry. After all, God affirms Job's response to his pain but condemns the mechanical theologizing of the friends. Many of the Psalms similarly cry out to God amid despair and struggle, and these are examples and prayers that we should take note of.

We have seen in Job's story how suffering confronts him with the shadow side of his personality. Many of us live completely unaware in this regard, but we don't have to. We need to learn to know ourselves and to actively work on coming to grips with who we are and the shadow sides of our strengths. We know that God wants to make us holy, whole human beings, and we can work with the Spirit in this respect by proactively attending to our own growth and development. This relates to all aspects of our personhood. The Dutch art historian Hans Rookmaker asked, "Why does God save us?" And he perceptively answered, "To make us fully human." Too much of church life today advocates a sort of Christianity that ignores our humanity. But holiness is about becoming the sort of people God wants us to be in all areas of our lives. Irenaeus famously said, "The glory of God is the human person fully alive!" We need to rehabilitate a vocabulary of "sanctification" in our churches with a biblical understanding of holiness as becoming fully human—as God intends us to be.

As noted above, the experience of suffering is one of terrible aloneness. Suffering is unique and individual, but the very fact that we have Job in our Bibles is a reminder that we are not alone; others have been where we are, and we can learn from them, finding hope in their stories.

The Christian tradition—unlike too much modern, superficial Christianity—is

> The experience of suffering is one of terrible aloneness. Suffering is unique and individual, but the very fact that we have Job in our Bibles is a reminder that we are not alone.

well acquainted with the role of suffering in the Christian life. I have already mentioned St. John of the Cross' *Dark Night of the Soul*, and good spiritual directors will have a wealth of experience about how to journey through the dark night. There is also a wealth of good literature, including narratives by those who have suffered terribly and come through the other side. C. S. Lewis suffered greatly when his wife died of cancer, and his book, *A Grief Observed*, is a rich resource for living through such pain.[3] Nicholas Wolterstorff lost one of his adult sons in a mountain climbing accident and ended up writing *Lament for a Son*, a book that many have found helpful in their own painful times.

Jerry Sittser was a young professor, and his wife homeschooled their children. They were studying native culture and went one afternoon to visit a native settlement. On their return journey, they had a head-on collision with a drunk, native driver. Jerry's mother, wife, and one of his children were killed. In *A Grace Disguised*, he describes how at a certain point he had to consciously enter the darkness of his horrific experience with no idea where it would take him. Years later, Jerry is able to look back and use the word "grace" for his suffering.

In his biographical work,[4] the novelist Frederick Buechner describes how the whole of his life opens up from the suicide of his father when he was a young child. Author Henri Nouwen also suffered a lot in his life, and his gift was to write honestly about his experiences. After his restless heart finally found a home at the L'Arche house in Toronto, his great need for deep relationship reached crisis point and he suffered a major breakdown. From that experience, he wrote his exquisite book, *The Inner Voice of Love: A Journey through Anguish to Freedom.*

Christians are certainly not exempt from suffering, and in the tradition we find rich resources to help in times of trouble. Just knowing that others have been where we are can help, as does learning how they gradually found their way through and were deeply formed in the process.

Perhaps one of the most extraordinary affirmations of grace and God's providence in suffering is that of the 20th-century Japanese Christian Takashi Nagai. Nagai was an adult convert to Christianity and became part of a vital Christian community in Japan that had suffered terrible persecution over the centuries. He was a doctor, a radiologist, a professor, a husband, and a father. He was in Nagasaki on the day the atom bomb was dropped on the city. Nagai's wife, Midori, and many, many others died instantly or later from the terrible radiation. At least 8,000 Christians died in the blast. The cathedral in Nagasaki was destroyed, and Nagai was asked to speak at the requiem mass for the dead held in its ashes. He thought hard about what to say. In his speech, he noted that on the morning of August 9, 1945, the Supreme Council of War was in session to decide whether to surrender or to continue fighting. At 11:02 the atom bomb fell on Nagasaki. At that same time, the Emperor of Japan asserted himself and declared his decision to surrender unconditionally. The Imperial Rescript was promulgated on August 15, ending the fighting. Nagai noted that August 15 was also the Feast of the Assumption of Mary. He suggested that this convergence of events

was "the mysterious Providence of God" and goes on
to argue that:

> God's Providence chose Urakami and car-
> ried the bomb right above our homes.
> Is there not a profound relationship be-
> tween the annihilation of Nagasaki and the
> end of the war? Was not Nagasaki the cho-
> sen victim, the lamb without blemish, slain
> as a whole burnt offering on an altar of sac-
> rifice, atoning for the sins of all the nations
> during World War II?[5]

Nagai died from exposure to radiation, but in his
final years, he bore a truly extraordinary witness to
God and his love. He wrote a series of books and lived
a life of simplicity and service to the end. As Paul Ham
says, "Nagai's faith would survive the toughest tests
which God had set before Job."[6]

The extraordinary message of Job is that deep suffering is graced. Generally, we only see this in retro-
spect—once we or someone we know has emerged out
of the darkness—and it is unhelpful to keep telling
people this when they are in the midst of hell. But the
book of Job makes clear that Job's suffering was graced.
Buechner expresses this beautifully:

> As for the children he had lost when the
> house blew down, not to mention all his em-
> ployees, he never got an explanation about
> them because he never asked for one, and
> the reason he never asked for one was that
> he knew that even if God gave him one that
> made splendid sense out of all the pain and

suffering that had ever been since the world
began, it was no longer splendid sense that
he needed because with his own eyes he
had beheld, and not as a stranger, the one
who in the end clothed all things, no mat-
ter how small or confused or in pain, with
his own splendor. And that was more than
sufficient.[7]

He had seen the great glory, so shot through
with sheer, fierce light and life and gladness,
had heard the great voice raised in song so
full of terror and wildness and beauty, that
from that moment on, nothing else mattered. All possible questions melted like
mist, and all possible explanations withered like grass.[8]

Suffering led Job into a much deeper experience of
God and in the process formed him into a wiser and
better man. Although suffering is always a mystery,
Job's sort of suffering has the uncanny habit of going
after the bull's-eye of a person's life, attending to
those areas that really need transformation. Genesis
22 recounts a similar and harrowing story of Abraham,
who was told to go and
sacrifice his son Isaac.
In order to be worthy of
the covenant, Abraham
had to be willing to re-
linquish the covenant,
as embodied in Isaac.

> Job's sort of suffering
> has the uncanny habit of
> going after the bull's eye
> of a person's life, attending
> to those areas that really
> need transformation.

There *is* evil in suffering; hence the role of Satan in Job 1–2. But evil has a habit of overreaching itself, and Satan would never have guessed how Job would turn out in the end—more mature, wiser, and blessed. Books like Job enable us, albeit with difficulty, to face the worst forms of suffering, in all their horror and agony and mystery, and yet to emerge from the depths and to be able to say with Julian of Norwich, "All will be well, and all manner of things will be well."

We should also note that counselors are fashioned through the furnace of suffering. Nouwen wrote a book called *The Wounded Healer*. Wounds are messy things, and most of us would rather run 1,000 miles than face our smelly, disgusting wounds. Ironically, however, wounds are the place of growth, and we will never be good counselors—people who can bring healing into the lives of others—without having lived our own wounds through to healing. We want good pastors and counselors, but let us remember, that we will only get such when they are granted the space to go through the furnace of formation.

**SUGGESTED READING**

☐   Job 29–30

☐   Read one of the books mentioned above and compare that author's story to Job's.

## Reflection

Far too many of us live relatively unconscious of the forces and people that have shaped us into who we are.

A useful exercise is to map out or draw the major contours of our life stories.

Are you familiar with the difference between suffering in which you experience God's presence and suffering in which God feels completely absent?

_____

_____

_____

Why do you think God sometimes withdraws from us in times when we feel we need him most?

_____

_____

_____

In terms of what we can learn from Job, which areas do you most need to attend to?

_____

_____

_____

How do you plan to do this?

_____

_____

_____

# 9

# CONCLUSION

As Kierkegaard so clearly knew, we need the book of Job! Sadly, it is not a book that is well-known or much read, studied, or preached on by Christians today. That is greatly to our loss and needs to change. My hope is that this book will contribute to such a recovery. Job has important lessons for those of us who suffer and for those of us who counsel those who suffer. When we really, really want to yell at God, Job is there for us. For those who suffer profoundly, Job is a reminder that in our darkest hours God is present and at work, even though we have absolutely no idea what he is up to and even if it feels as though the world and God have gone mad. For those who counsel, Job calls us to discern when repentance is required and when God is deeply at work in ways we do not understand. In the latter context, the worst thing a counselor can do is to offer quick solutions; rather, a wise counselor should provide support when possible and wait with the sufferer to

> For those who suffer profoundly, Job is a reminder that in our darkest hours God is present and at work.

see what God will bring to pass. It *will* pass, and with James we will find ourselves saying, "See what God has wrought!"

> **SUGGESTED READING**
>
> ☐   Make time to become familiar with Job.
>      Read it slowly and attentively.

## Reflection

How has Job spoken to you over the time you have spent with it?

_____

_____

Are there lessons you should not forget?

_____

_____

_____

## Further Reading

☐   Read and reread Job. There is no alternative to immersing ourselves in the actual text.

☐   The best recent commentary on Job is, in my opinion: Lindsay Wilson, *Job*. 2 Horizons OTC. (Grand Rapids: Eerdmans, 2015).

☐   Craig G. Bartholomew and Ryan O'Dowd, *Old Testament Wisdom: A Theological Introduction*

(Nottingham: Apollos; Downers Grove, Ill.: IVP Academic, 2011) may also be a useful resource.

☐ Do consult the many useful resources in the *Lexham Bible Dictionary*. Check it out at LexhamBibleDictionary.com.

☐ Read stories of people who have suffered and how they have found God in the midst of such experiences.

# FEARING GOD IN THE OLD TESTAMENT

**Miles Custis**

Fearing God is an important concept in the OT. While "fear" can describe terror or dread (Gen 3:10), the OT use of "fear" often indicates awe or reverence. To fear God is to express loyalty to him and faithfulness to his covenant. Those who fear God exhibit trust in him and obedience to his commandments. According to the OT, those who fear God obtain God's protection, wisdom, and blessing.

## Response to Holiness

The fear of God is often evoked in response to God's holiness (Exod 3:5–6; Isa 8:13). For example, the biblical writers describe God and his name as holy and "awesome" (Psa 111:9). The term "awesome" translates the word *nora*, a form of the word *yara* which means "to fear." The fear of God is also related to God's greatness (Deut 7:21; Psa 99:3); people fear God because of his mighty deeds (Exod 15:11). For example, the

Israelites respond to God's saving power in bringing them out of Egypt by fearing him (Exod 14:30–31).

## Obedience

The biblical texts often parallel the fear of God with obedience. For example, in Gen 22:12, God recognizes Abraham's obedience to sacrifice Isaac as fear of him. The link between fearing God and obedience appears throughout Deuteronomy, where fearing God and keeping his commandments are closely linked (Deut 5:29; 8:6; 10:12–13). In the OT, people demonstrate fear of God by obeying the Law (Deut 6:2). Likewise, obedience to the Law teaches people to fear God (Deut 4:10; 14:23; 17:19; 31:12–13).

Fearing God is also related to obedience in Leviticus, specifically regarding social relations. For example, Leviticus states that, instead of wronging others (Lev 25:17) by doing things like cursing the deaf and blind (Lev 19:14), people should fear God. The text of Leviticus further associates the fear of God with honoring the elderly (Lev 19:32), forgoing the charging of interest (Lev 25:36), and treating servants kindly (Lev 25:43).

## Loyalty and Faithfulness

The fear of God is also closely tied to loyalty and faithfulness to God (2 Chr 19:6). For instance, after the people of Israel conquered the land of Canaan, Joshua charged them to faithfully fear God by serving him alone and putting away other gods (Josh 24:14–15). In 2 Kings 17:35–39, the fear of God describes loyalty to him in contrast to worshipping other gods.

## Fear of God in Prophetic Literature and Psalms

The prophets equate fearing God with a pious attitude toward him; fearing God is linked to honoring God (Isa 8:13) and obeying his commands (Isa 50:10). The prophets often criticize the Israelites for forsaking the fear of God (Jer 2:19; 3:8; Mal 3:5); when speaking of restoration, they include a restoration of the fear of God among God's people (Isa 59:19; Jer 32:39–40; Hos 3:5).

In the Psalms, fearing God is often likened to trusting God (Pss 40:4; 115:11). The designation of "those who fear God" is used to refer to the community of those faithful to him (Pss 22:25; 66:16). Those who fear God receive protection, deliverance, and blessing (Pss 25:12–13; 31:19; 34:7, 9; 85:9; 111:5; 115:13; 145:19). They also enjoy a close relationship with God (Pss 25:14; 33:18). The Psalms likewise equate worship and praise with the fear of God (Pss 5:7; 22:23; 135:20).

## Fear of God in Wisdom Literature

The fear of God also appears as a central theme of Wisdom literature, where it several times refers to the beginning of wisdom or knowledge (Prov 1:7; 9:10; Psa 111:10). Proverbs classifies those without a fear of God as haters of knowledge (Prov 1:29). Proverbs also relates the fear of God to humility and righteous living (Prov 3:7; 8:13; 14:2; 16:6; 22:4). Fearing God also leads to blessing and long life (Prov 10:27; 14:26–27; 19:23; 28:14). Like obedience, the relationship between fearing God and wisdom is cyclical: Fearing God results in wisdom (Prov 15:33), and receiving wisdom helps people understand the fear of God (Prov 2:1–5).

The book of Job describes Job as someone who fears God (Job 1:1; 1:8; 2:3). In fact, Job's fear of God is the focal point of the book, as Satan questions Job's reason for fearing God (Job 1:9). The book of Ecclesiastes concludes with an exhortation to "fear God and keep his commandments" (Eccl 12:13). It also notes that God acts in order that people may fear him (Eccl 3:14).[1]

# SATAN IN THE OLD TESTAMENT AND THE SERPENT OF GENESIS 3

### Michael S. Heiser

We typically understand the serpent (*nachash*) of Gen 3 as Satan in the guise of a snake—that is, as a member of the animal kingdom. And we usually think of Satan as the devil. But is this biblical? In Rev 12:9; 20:2, the serpent (*nachash*) from Eden is associated with the devil, and the devil with Satan. But Revelation is the last book of the NT, and was most likely written a full 50 years after the earthly ministry of Jesus. Further, the term "devil"—which derives from the Greek word *diabolos*—does not appear in the OT. Prior to Revelation, the Bible never associates the serpent of Genesis with Satan.

By understanding how the serpent was conceived in OT thinking, we can better understand the development of Revelation's view of Satan. By examining what the Hebrew term *satan* means in the OT, we'll find that the very late correlation of the serpent with Satan (and the devil) does not contradict OT theology—but neither does it define the OT view. Rather, OT biblical theology creates a theological framework in which the later NT convergence of these figures into an archenemy of God makes sense.

## Satan in the Old Testament

The Hebrew word *satan* is not a proper noun in the OT. As such, the term was not used to refer to a cosmic archenemy of God. A brief consideration of the Hebrew grammar helps explain why.

Like English, Hebrew does not attach the definite article ("the") to proper personal nouns. For example, English speakers do not refer to themselves (or to another person) with phrases like "the Tom" or "the Janet." However, most of the 27 occurrences of *satan* in the Hebrew Bible include a definite article—essentially reading "the *satan*." For example, all occurrences in the book of Job (Job 1:6–9, 12; 2:1–4, 6–7) include the definite article. The term is applied to a divine being with the definite article in Zech 3:1–2, where Joshua the high priest stands before the *satan* who accuses him of misdeeds in the company of the Angel of Yahweh. Yahweh then rebukes the *satan*, since he has pardoned Joshua (and so, Israel).

Of the remaining occurrences of *satan*, only three passages use the word of a divine being: Num 22:22, 32 and 1 Chr 21:1. The rest are used of humans. In these three passages, a definite article is not included—meaning that there is no *grammatical* reason to prohibit them from referring to God's archenemy. Yet the

context of each of these passages rules out this interpretation. In fact, the two occurrences in Numbers
refer not to God's enemy, but to the Angel of Yahweh.
The remaining occurrence—where the *satan* provokes
David to take a census—also does not refer to God's
archenemy: in the parallel passage to the event (2 Sam
24:1), God himself prompts David to take the census;
and contextual clues in 1 Chr 21:1 indicate that the *satan* is the Angel of Yahweh. Thus the two passages can
be harmonized, as the OT often co-identifies God and
the Angel of Yahweh (see 1 Chr 21:1). Ultimately, there
are no passages in the OT where the word *satan* refers
to God's divine archenemy.

But why is the word *satan* used to refer to humans
and the Angel of Yahweh? The answer is straightforward: the term means "accuser" or "challenger." *Satan*
describes a particular action or role, often in the context of opposition or judgment. In the case of Num
22:22, 32, God sent the Angel of Yahweh to oppose
Balaam on his journey to curse Israel. In the case of
1 Chr 21:1, the parallel passage of 2 Sam 24:1 explains:
"The anger of the LORD was kindled against Israel, and
he incited David against them, saying, 'Go, number
Israel and Judah.' " God was already angry at David
and planned to judge him. He then sent the Angel to
prompt David to take a census, which led to his punishment. God used the Angel (his accuser) as an in-
strument of judgment on David.

## The Serpent in Genesis

The word *satan* does not occur anywhere in Gen
3; rather, the word translated "serpent" is *nachash*.
Hence, the two terms are never co-identified in the

Old Testament. But just because the serpent (*nachash*) is not called *satan* does not mean that the serpent was not a divine being. *Satan* may refer to either a human or a divine being, depending on the context. Likewise, *nachash*—though typically referring to a snake—has nuances which allow for multiple meanings.

When *nachash* functions as a noun, it means "snake." But the root consonants of the word also form the Hebrew verb that means "to conjure" or "practice divination" (see 2 Kgs 21:6; Gen 30:27; 44:5). *Nachash* in Gen 3 can be interpreted in this light, and understood as "the conjurer." Since the practice of divination aimed to solicit and dispense divine knowledge, the context of Gen 3 is consistent with this possibility. However, technical grammatical reasons make this interpretation unlikely.

The root is also the basis for words that refer to shining metals, such as bronze—a description used elsewhere in the OT for divine beings (see Ezek 1:14–16, 27–28; Dan 10:6; compare Matt 28:3; Rev 10:1). For example, Ezekiel 28:13 contains an "anointed cherub" figure, who inhabits the garden of Eden. If this figure is a divine being, there may be a link between that figure's brilliant, shining appearance and the root of *nachash* in Gen 3. Consequently, the word *nachash* may refer to a "shining one" in the Garden of Eden—a divine being who conversed with Eve and deceived her.

Since Eden was God's temple and abode, the "shining one" option represents a viable interpretation. It also helps explain why Eve is not surprised when the *nachash* speaks to her. The primary obstacle to this perspective is the possible inter-relationship between Gen 3, Ezek 28, and Isa 14: Both Ezekiel and

Isaiah describe Eden and the cosmic rebellion without reference to a snake.

## New Testament Conflation of These Terms

In the book of Revelation, the term *satan* and the serpent (*nachash*) of Gen 3 are conceptually merged. The correlation is logical: The serpent was the original "opposer" ("adversary"; *satan*) of God's kingdom on earth. As such, the *nachash* was perceived as the original enemy, the Grand Adversary (*satan*). However, when this correlation developed is less apparent. A number of non-biblical Jewish writings prior to the birth of Jesus developed a rich tradition about the Grand Adversary. Some of these texts used "Satan" as a proper noun in referring to that enemy; NT writers did as well. Many of these non-biblical texts were associated with conceptions of apocalypse, as is the book of Revelation.[1]

# NOTES

## Chapter 1. Introduction

1. See Craig G. Bartholomew, *Reading Proverbs with Integrity* (Cambridge: Grove, 2001). See also Michael V. Fox, *Proverbs 1–9* (Anchor Yale Bible 18A; New Haven: Yale University Press, 2000), 91–92. This theology is sometimes labeled "mechanical retribution."

2. See Bartholomew, *Reading Proverbs with Integrity*.

## Chapter 2. The Portrait of Job

1. See Michael Fishbane, "Jeremiah IV 23–26 and Job III 3–13: A Recovered Use of the Creation Pattern," *VT* 21 (1971): 151–67. See also Robert S. Fyall, *Now My Eyes Have Seen You: Images of Creation and Evil in the Book of Job* (Downers Grove, Ill.: InterVarsity, 2002), 102ff.

## Chapter 3. The Portraits of God among Job's Friends

1. See Sheila Cassidy, *Audacity to Believe: An Autobiography* (London: Collins, 1977).

2. Édouard Dhorme, *A Commentary on the Book of Job* (Nashville, Tenn.: Thomas Nelson, 1984 [original 1926]), cxxxv.

## Chapter 4. Job's View of God

1. Alvin Plantinga, *Warranted Christian Belief* (New York: OUP, 2000) 496–98. See also Eleonore Stump, *Walking in Darkness: Narrative and the Problem of Suffering* (Oxford and New York: OUP, 2010), 177–26.

2. Quoted by Harold Bloom, ed., *The Book of Job* (New York: Chelsea House, 1988), 2.

3. Plantinga, ibid., 497.

4. For further discussion, see Craig G. Bartholomew and Ryan O'Dowd. *Old Testament Wisdom Literature: A Theological Introduction* (Downers Grove, Ill.: InterVarsity Press, 2011), ch. 6.

5. Robert Alter, *The Art of Biblical Poetry* (Edinburgh: T&T Clark, 1985), 90.

6. Lindsay Wilson, *Job*. (2HOTC; Grand Rapids, Mich.: Eerdmans, 2015).

7. Robert Alter, *The World of Biblical Literature* (London: SPCK, 1992), 188–89.

8. Michael Fox, "Job 38 and God's Rhetoric" *Semeia* 19 (1981): 53–61.

9. See Fyall, *Now My Eyes Have Seen You*, 127–74, who uses ANE Canaanite mythology to argue that the Behemoth and Leviathan sustain the presence of death, evil, and the Satan figure from chapters 1–2.

10. Alter, *The World of Biblical Literature*, 189.

11. The image of the bucket and torchlight comes from Karl Popper, *Objective Knowledge: An Evolutionary Approach* (Oxford: Clarendon, 1972), 341–61.

12. Job also uses this verb in 31:13 where he claims not to have "rejected" his servants.

13. F. I. Anderson, *Job: An Introduction and Commentary*. (TOTC; Leicester, UK: IVP, 1976), 292.

## Chapter 5. The Power of Poetry

1. Alter, *The Art of Biblical Poetry*, 89.

2. Ibid., 92.

3. Ibid., 90.

4. For further reading, see Craig G. Bartholomew and Ryan O'Dowd, *Old Testament Wisdom: A Theological Introduction* (Nottingham: Apollos; Downers Grove, Ill.: IVP Academic, 2011), 47–72.

5. The word for "darken" in the Hebrew can also mean "confuse" or "obscure."

6. George Steiner, *The Death of Tragedy* (New York: Oxford University Press, 1961), 4.

7. Martha Nussbaum, *The Fragility of Goodness: Luck and Ethics in Greek Tragedy and Philosophy* (2d ed.; Cambridge: Cambridge University Press, 2001), 186.

8. Ibid., 378–85.

9. Ibid., 378–94.

10. Peter J. Leithart, *Deep Comedy: Trinity, Tragedy, and Hope in Western Literature* (Moscow, Idaho: Canon Press, 2006), 25.

11. In James F. Sennett, ed., *The Analytic Theist: An Alvin Plantinga Reader* (Grand Rapids, Mich.: Eerdmans, 1998), 339.

12. Bernard Williams, *Shame and Necessity* (Berkeley, Calif.: University of California Press, 1993). William's realism leaves us, however, resigned to our lack of control over much of life. Nussbaum, in *Fragility of Goodness*, attempts to move this in a more positive direction by arguing that such realism enables us to accept what we cannot change while actively engaging the ethical space we find ourselves in. However, this is proposed in the context of her move to affirm the Enlightenment goal of "a social life grounded in reason" and her acknowledgement that, "Few of us now believe that we live in a world that is providentially ordered for the sake of the overall good; few even believe in a teleology of human social life moving toward greater perfection" (*Fragility of Goodness*, xvi, xv). It is hard to see how hopeful such a vision actually is, and one also wonders how Nussbaum can be so certain that so "few" believe these things amid a worldwide resurgence of religion.

13. Alter, *The Art of Biblical Poetry*, 87.

14. Alter, *The World of Biblical Literature*, 188–89.

15. For a sample of modern views, see Kathryn Schifferdecker, *Out of the Whirlwind: Creation Theology in the Book of Job* (Harvard Theological Studies 61; Cambridge: Cambridge University Press, 2008), 5–11.

16. Jon D. Levenson, review of C. A. Newsom, *The Book of Job: A Contest of Moral Imaginations*, *JR* 84 (2004): 271–72.

17. Job parodies Psalm 8 in Job 7:17–21.

18.  Rolf P. Knierim, *The Task of Old Testament Theology: Method and Cases* (Grand Rapids, Mich.: Eerdmans, 1995), 202.

19.  Frederick Buechner, *Peculiar Treasures: A Biblical Who's Who* (San Francisco, Calif.: HarperSanFrancisco, 1979), 75.

20. Buechner, *Peculiar Treasures*, 76–77.

## Chapter 6. Job's Journey of Transformation

1.  Ellen F. Davis, *Scripture, Culture, and Agriculture: An Agrarian Reading of the Bible* (Cambridge: Cambridge University Press, 2008).

2. Analysis of the stages in the grief process are another helpful means of analyzing Job, but they lack the transformative element in Jung's psychology.

3. Susannah Ticciati, *Job and the Disruption of Identity: Reading beyond Barth* (London/New York: T&T Clark, 2005).

4. Edward F. Edinger, *Ego and Archetype: Individuation and the Religious Formation of the Psyche* (Boston, Mass.: Shambhala, 1992), 76–96. In terms of the historicity of Job, it is intriguing to note that Edinger regards Job as likely reflecting the actual experience of an individual. He sees the friends as an example of *active imagination* by the individual and suggests that the three-plus-one friends implies resolution—so that Elihu's contribution should be read as an anticipation of the resolution of Job's suffering. On the role of the three and the four, see Edinger, ibid., 179–93.

5. Edinger, *Ego and Archetype*, 7.

6. Ibid., 37.

7. Carl. G. Jung, *Mysterium Coniunctionis* (Collected Works 14; Princeton: Princeton University Press, 1966–1979), 778.

8. David Bakan, *Disease, Pain and Sacrifice: Toward a Theology of Suffering* (Chicago: University of Chicago Press, 1968), 72. Bakan argues, "Pain is the demand on the conscious ego to work to bring the decentralized part back into the unity of the organism. Pain is the imperative to the ego to assume the responsibility of telic centralization, the ego itself having emerged as a result of telic decentralization."

9. St. John of the Cross, *The Dark Night of the Soul* (3d ed.; London: Burns & Oates, 1976), refers repeatedly to Job.

10. See Leo G. Perdue, *Wisdom Literature: A Theological History* (Louisville, Ky.: WJK Press, 2007), 98–102; Fishbane, "Jeremiah IV 23–26 and Job III 3–13: A Recovered Use of the Creation Pattern."

11. Alter, *The Art of Biblical Poetry*, 96.

12. Schifferdecker, *Out of the Whirlwind*, 67–68.

13. Edinger, ibid., 80.

14. Ibid., 91. Italics my own.

15. T. S. Eliot, *Four Quartets*, "Little Gidding" V.

16. Edinger, ibid.

## Chapter 7. Job and Jesus

1. Karl Barth, *CD* (IV.3.1; §70), 368–478.

## Chapter 8. The Reader's Journey of Transformation

1. Søren Kierkegaard, *Fear and Trembling/Repetition* (trans. H. V. and E. H. Hong; Princeton: Princeton University Press, 1983), 204–05.

2. See Eugene H. Peterson, *Working the Angles: The Shape of Pastoral Integrity* (Grand Rapid, Mich.: Eerdmans, 1987), for a discussion of the practice of spiritual direction.

3. C. S. Lewis, *A Grief Observed* (London: Faber & Faber, 1961).

4. Frederick Buechner, *The Sacred Journey: A Memoir of Early Days* (New York: Harpercollins, 1982). See also ibid., *Now and Then* (New York: HarperOne, 1991); *Telling Secrets* (New York: HarperOne, 1991); *The Eyes of the Heart* (New York: HarperOne, 1999).

5. Quoted in Paul Glynn's extraordinary book, *A Song for Nagasaki: The Story of Takashi Nagai: Scientist, Convert, and Survivor of the Atomic Bomb* (San Francisco, Calif.: Ignatius, 1988), 188.

6. Paul Ham, *Hiroshima Nagasaki: The Real Story of the Atomic Bombings and Their Aftermath* (London: Transworld, 2011), 59.

7.  Buechner, *Peculiar Treasures*, 77.

8.  Buechner, *Peculiar Treasures*, 76.

## Appendix A. Fearing God in the Old Testament

1.  Miles Custis, "Fearing God in the Old Testament," in *Faithlife Study Bible* (ed. John D. Barry, Michael R. Grigoni, Michael S. Heiser, Miles Custis, Douglas Mangum, and Matthew M. Whitehead, Bellingham, Wash.: Lexham Press, 2012).

## Appendix B. Satan in the Old Testament and the Serpent of Genesis 3

1.  Michael S. Heiser, "Satan in the Old Testament and the Serpent of Genesis 3," in *Faithlife Study Bible* (ed. John D. Barry, Michael R. Grigoni, Michael S. Heiser, Miles Custis, Douglas Mangum, and Matthew M. Whitehead, Bellingham, Wash.: Lexham Press, 2012).

Printed in the United States
by Baker & Taylor Publisher Services